Starfish on a Beach:

THE PANDEMIC POEMS

Starfish on a Beach:

THE PANDEMIC POEMS

MARGARET RANDALL

WingsPress

San Antonio, Texas
2020

First Edition
ISBN: 978-1-60940-615-8

E-books:
ISBN: 978-1-60940-616-5

Wings Press
P.O. Box 591176
San Antonio, Texas 78259

Wings Press books are distributed to the trade by
Independent Publishers Group
www.ipgbook.com

Due to the 2020 pandemic, no Library of Congress
cataloging-in-publication data was available.

Acknowledgements

As the coronavirus pandemic unfolded, many of these poems
were posted on Margaret Randall's Facebook page. Some also
appeared, either in English or Spanish or both, in: *Altazor*
(Chile), *Revista Casa de las Américas* (Cuba), *Rio Grande Review,*
and *Tricontinental Newsletter* (United States).

Contents

These poems are not for the dead but for those who survived

this time around, for the dead have lived their lives

while the survivors must live with their loss.

INTRODUCTION

I wrote these poems during the extraordinary time between March and May 2020, when the world suddenly found itself in a situation without modern precedent. A new and virulent viral infection called COVID-19 and popularly referred to as the coronavirus began in the Chinese city of Wuhan and made its way across the globe. Before travel restrictions, quarantines and other precautionary measures could be established, great numbers of people were infected in Iran, South Korea, Japan, Italy, the United States, and eventually almost every nation on earth. Then the death toll began mounting, mounting. By early April 100,000 world-wide were presumed to have died but we knew this number represented a fraction of those who had succumbed to the virus; without sufficient test kits or the time to evaluate every victim, it was impossible to know. When you read this, these numbers will have increased many times over.

Depending on their willingness to listen to the scientists, governments addressed the menace differently. Some, besieged by fundamentalist ignorance and misplaced allegiances, failed to take action until large numbers of their citizens were ill and dying, their medical facilities were overwhelmed and their economies in freefall. The more scientifically oriented governments acted immediately and appropriately and were able to contain the invisible terror, at least on their home ground. But our world today is connected in so many different ways that the actions of the larger more powerful nations inevitably affect the entire world.

Within each country people also suffered varying degrees of risk. The elderly and those with underlying health issues were judged most vulnerable. But class and culture also influenced who would get sick and where. People of color were infected at much higher rates than mainstream white populations. As always, the poor were the most exposed and unprotected. Those without homes endured added misery. Prisoners warehoused in crowded unsanitary conditions knew they had little hope. Refugees condemned to the camps on our southern border were abandoned to an uncertainty worse than they'd already known. As always, those with access had a better chance of surviving while "throwaway" populations were doomed.

As businesses were forced to close, hourly wage earners lost jobs they may never get back. Tens of thousands of small enterprises may be shuttered forever. Government aid packages and subsidies went to corporations deemed "too big to fail."

If you fell ill with something other than the virus it was almost impossible for you to be seen by a healthcare professional. All procedures deemed optional were cancelled for the duration. In many places, abortion was labeled one of these: conservative public officials were quick to take advantage of the crisis to limit democratic practices. And in facilities overwhelmed with victims of the virus doctors and nurses were called upon to work intolerable hours and often lacked the resources they needed to treat their patients. Many of them got ill and died. Healthcare personnel also had to begin choosing who would live and who die. Triage became trauma.

In the United States the crisis coincided with the presidency of Donald Trump, a sociopath known for his racism and xenophobia, erratic behavior, refusal to listen to those who know, and his self-serving political machinations. From the beginning, his failure to recognize the crisis for what it was and lack of leadership cost tens of thousands of lives. Many state governors and other elected officials, on the other hand, demonstrated great ability and compassion in a situation for which they were totally unprepared and weren't getting the support they needed from the federal government. In a more intimate sense, individuals were generally kind to one another, noticing who needed help and providing it generously.

We remembered the 1918 Spanish flu and other worldwide epidemics. But the world has changed dramatically in the past century and both risk and containment posed very different challenges now. Some likened the emergency to European fascism at mid-twentieth century, the Cambodian Killing Fields, 9/11, or situations provoked by major earthquakes, floods and fires. This emergency was everywhere, though, and comparisons meant little.

Some countries acted not only quickly and efficiently but also with great demonstrations of solidarity. No sooner was it evident that measures never before taken would have to be implemented, China immediately constructed and outfitted several immense hospitals. It implemented strict containment policies and demanded obedience from its citizens. And as soon as it had its own problem under control, the Chinese government began sending planeloads of trained personnel and medical equipment abroad. Cuba, too, showed its long-practiced solidarity, delivering doctors and disinfection systems to countries in need. Cuba's free and universal healthcare system, in place for decades, limited the spread of the virus in-country.

US Americans were told to stay home, self-isolate, disinfect our homes and clothing; and when we had to go out wear facemasks and gloves and practice what was called "social distancing," meaning staying six feet away from others. We didn't know if these measures would be effective; scientists were racing to understand the virus's characteristic and recommendations were often contradictory. Anyone who could, worked from home. For many, in this time of digital options, this was possible. Many more were simply furloughed or fired. Schools and universities closed, there were no university graduating classes of 2020, and the hopes of a generation were erased in what seemed like a single stroke. The emergency aid package voted on by Congress and signed into law by the president, favored corporations over the working man or woman. Life for most of the world's inhabitants will never be the same, either because they lost one or more loved ones to the pandemic or because their economic futures were changed irrevocably.

I stayed home and wrote poems. They emerged in a torrent, one after another, sometimes three or more in a single day. I present them here, not in the order in which they were written but arranged and revised as the crisis took shape and took over. They are one poet's witness to an extraordinary time.

Margaret Randall
Albuquerque, New Mexico
May 2020

Starfish on a Beach:

THE PANDEMIC POEMS

COVID-19

When the death toll is expected
to be in the millions
chances are
someone you love will die.

The plagues of old revisit us now
and we scramble
to stay safe, stay sane
and present for others,

help neighbors, buy only
what we need
from store shelves emptying
to a beat of fear.

Let us share facemasks
like the Chinese
and wash our hands
in silent prayer.

Let us sing from balconies
imagined and real
like Italians
in nationwide lockdown.

Let us be kind to one another
and organize the remedies
and solutions
irresponsible leaders put at risk.

If this is the Big One,
let us go out
in dignity, if a rehearsal
let us finally propose to live in peace.

We Do Not Know

Some point to reduced CO2, wildlife
returning to lands where humans
don't crowd them out.
Some foretell end times, apocalyptic
prophesies announcing

a doom we deserve because
we have sinned
in the eyes of some vengeful God,
are queer or freethinking
or simply believe in science.

The truth is, we do not know how this crisis
will end or what will be left
when it stops breathing down our necks,
threatening every inhalation
with unseen droplets of infection.

We want to paint a picture of hope, avoid
despair alongside sickness and death.
We want to believe this terror
will change our future for the better.
We just don't know.

What we do know is words have meanings
and we must aim our messages
straight as arrows
into the hearts of those who hope
to profit from this pain.

A Picture is Worth

Mountainsides giving way beneath
the rains, leaving nothing
but gaping holes where houses stood
and people lived.

Fires roaring across forested landscape
in northern California
erasing in hours
towns with names like Paradise.

Where seas retreat from shore
then barrel inland again
corpses float in photographs
that stop our breath.

And where human migration
is the tragedy
empty life jackets
stand in for corpses.

This pandemic, with its invisible
globules hanging for days
in air that looks the same as it did
yesterday and the day before

doesn't confront us with pictures
that scream holocaust, take me
seriously, act now or sicken
and die.

Its brutal images will come later,
too few to prod us
to action, too late for all those
sacrificed:

a New York subway car with one
rider, a single pigeon
in Vatican Square, bodies stored
in an ice-skating rink.

Act now, decisively, without such
visuals leading the way,
before the advice that should
have been our first defense.

Our Resolve Must Be Stronger

We are all at risk: the rich and poor
despite Miguel Barbosa, foolish
governor of the state of Puebla, Mexico,
who claims only the rich will fall ill,
the poor are immune.

Despite our bumbling ranting US president
who insists on calling it the China virus,
not caring that his words
mean fear and danger for Asian Americans
all across this land.

Despite public figures who hug and kiss
on our TV screens, maintaining
love cures all, their images
setting a deadly example
of cultish ignorance.

This plague crosses every racial, class
and cultural line, attacks women
and men, old and young, those who
ascribe will to a God of their invention
and those who look to science.

It knows no borders, hovers unseen
waiting to enter eyes, noses,
mouths, along with that feelgood message

some intone that puts
us all at risk.

Our resolve must be stronger, sharper,
more intelligent and with memory
of past pandemics. Our actions
must reflect the wisdom of this century
in which we live and die.

Starfish on a Beach: A Fable for 2020

I think of a story Barbara used to tell, about a man stand-
ing on a beach scattered with hundreds of starfish. He
picked them up, one by one, and threw each back into the
sea. Another man walking by (such stories always seem to
feature men) stopped, watched for a while, then said: *You'll
never be able to throw them all back. Do you think what you're
doing really matters?* The first man picked up another star-
fish, tossed it into the waves and answered: *Mattered to that
one.*

I'm thinking of this story now in the context of
COVID-19, the plague that is sickening and killing
people around the world. I've heard it suggested,
both by those who believe in science and by Christian
or other fundamentalists that this is a culling. The
Earth is cleansing itself of overpopulation, ridding
itself of surplus humans, as it were. The fundamen-
talists would substitute the word God for the word
Earth.

Which leads to my next thought. Even if we can't
save everyone who gets sick, we must do our best
to protect as many as possible. It may not matter to
everyone, but it will surely matter to "that one."

Statistics

The pundits give us graphs,
projections with
different colored lines
representing China, Italy,
our own United States.

They move from left to right
rising gentle or dramatic
but too often in ascent,
giving us hope or telling us
we are headed for disaster.

Statistics have always been
suspect, coming
as they do from minds
endeavoring to comfort
or alarm.

Context is too often missing,
that terrain where
we may consider
time, space, imagination
or our own collective response

in this race to understand
what we should think
and how we must act
before the lines become
a web that traps us in its weave.

Beneath the Waves

This is a time when we
summon tears
that don't come,
grief lurking like the current
that pulls a body
beneath the waves.

This is a time when a smile
may not be a smile
even in translation
but a stand-in for where
our eyes would go if they
were open to a future tense.

Be afraid, very afraid: is the
mantra of those who
benefit from our despair.
Breathe, breathe deep
whisper those
who have been here before.

Fashioning Poems from the Trembling

Keep healthy, we tell one another,
stay safe,
take precautions,
do everything right.

We don't want to die
from this virus
but to make it through
without visible scars.

I want to make it through
with dignity as well,
my ideals still painted
billboard high.

I do not want to mark time
but use it well,
aim morsels of hope like paper cranes
soaring through infected air,

send kindness in every direction
and fashion poems
from the trembling
that would take us down.

Our Conversation has Changed

Our conversation has changed.
We are talking about
things we couldn't bring ourselves
to broach before.

If I get it, don't hook me up
to a ventilator...
I've had a good life...
Tell the children...

Experiencing the guilt of having
home and lover, imagining
those who lacked everything
before this plague,

we look into one another's eyes,
relieved to be facing
our deepest fears
in company.

The Quick Turn of a Screw

I have heard people say this worldwide pandemic
is changing everything.
Is it?
And if it is changing everything
will it change me? Will it change you?

If it does change us, in what ways
will we be different?
If we survive, will we be more optimistic?
If someone we loved dies, more pessimistic,
resigned or angry?

This virus didn't come with concentration camps
or ovens,
killing fields or mass disappearances.
The images it leaves
won't speak to generations.

We may marvel at its silence and suddenness,
like the quick turn of a screw
on an 18th century pillory
or the way a single hateful taunt
can provoke a suicide.

If we are changed, let it be for the better.
Let it be forever.
Let us not fall into our old ways,
coaxed back to them
by forgetting.

Who Knows How Many Socks and Scarves

Yeast and flour have vanished
from my grocer's shelves.
They say bakers are making
a lot of bread these days:
anxious hands kneading
our tension into dough.

Its scent lifts touch until
it fills a room,
pushing away
any threat to the lives
we make for ourselves
and those we love.

Those who knit click their
needles and those
who garden dip their hands
in soil. Who knows
how many socks and scarves
will come from this time of crisis?

I wonder what men are doing
to manage their fears
now that the gyms and bars
are closed
to say nothing of brothels
and private clubs.

Will this time of exceptionality
really have been exceptional?
Will it leave a closeness in its wake
or will we have taken
a step back in our Mars and Venus
struggle to know each other?

One-Part Dread to Two of Calm

Making my way across the debris field
separating sleep from
the high desert landscape of my day,
I ask myself the questions
that also plagued me yesterday:
Am I afraid? Will I venture outdoors?
Who should I call
and what can I do for those
more vulnerable than I?

I have no answers for these questions,
at least none that can flatten
the graph line of my anxiety,
help me feel better tomorrow
than today
or with more hope for rapid recovery.
There's still the persistent sniffle
released by Cottonwood seeds
carried on spring winds.

I ask my lungs if they are working
as they always have,
expanding and contracting
to a troubled beat.
I wonder if their effort is new
or familiar to a place
that only exists
in the perfect storm
of my invention.

One cup bleach to a gallon water,
one-part dread to two of calm,
more reason than fear
or fear than reason,
depending on the headlines,
most of which I know
I cannot not take as absolute truth
but must mix with a healthy dose
of critical thought.

I Miss

I miss the dinners with friends, sitting around
our table or theirs, sharing food
that speaks of long custom,
savors slow delight.

I miss our face to face conversations, connections
impossible to recreate on Skype
or telephone, words traveling
unimpeded among us.

I miss his hand on my shoulder, the way
her eyes met mine as we
reached to embrace
goodbye or hello.

I miss that easiness of living we've known,
we who do not live in prisons
or refugee camps, tent cities
or on the street.

This is a new sort of social loneliness
we must rigorously observe
if we hope once more to know the dinners,
conversations, comforting touch of a hand.

Clean

Did you wash that apple?
And what about the banana?
Well, since you throw away
the skin...
Yes, but you touch it
before you throw it away.

New conversations that fill
our days and dreams,
the nightmare beginning
where day ends, assuring
one another and ourselves
we are clean, clean, clean.

Better than Nothing

I don the cloth mask, couldn't locate
the N-95 I've been told
really keeps the hazardous mist
from nose and mouth, but cloth
is better than nothing
in this season of let's pretend.

Our hands are raw from the cleanser
in the dispenser at the supermarket
entrance. They must have made
the mix with too much alcohol,
so many ingredients
hard to come by these days.

These latex gloves chafe my hands
and make them sweat,
have given me a rash
that festers even
when I try to soothe it
with sterile lotion.

The solution you used to soak
the fruits and vegetables
makes this apple taste bitter
even though you peeled it
before cutting and arranging
the slices elegantly on the plate.

Presentation is important now that
our options for eating out
are reduced to pickups
at the curb.
Vital, though, to know
what we eat is clean.

At the end of the day we can
sleep peacefully,
dreaming of air
so fresh and plentiful
it would render a ventilator
obsolete.

Still, we may die of chemical poison
or protective gear
made in one of those other countries
we cannot trust because—you
know—they're just
not up to US standards.

State of Exception

It is an epidemic and then
a pandemic,
an outbreak in some reports,
a flareup or surge
when the numbers rise,
a leveling off
when they fall.

In some cities the numbers
double every week,
in others every day
or they may even triple
or quadruple
as more people are tested
and fiction becomes fact.

What we call the virus
is important
for getting us to take
it seriously or keeping us calm.
The message is everything
when advertising is the dogma
by which we live and die.

Perhaps we should pair
these names
with terms like nationalism,

class bias, race war, gender parity
and our unwillingness
to welcome those who come to us
escaping death by other means.

We must not allow
the facemask
to become a blindfold,
social distancing
to become disdain,
or a state of exception
to become our lives.

This Time No One Saw Coming

Ana in New York is working from home
and taking long walks.
In the center of the storm
she is going about a demanding life
steady on.

Ximena tells me she must walk her dog
three times a day in Mexico City.
He struggles against her
disinfecting his paws in a special bath
each time they return.

In Puebla preventative protocols
weren't yet in place
when Sarah joined other mourners
walking behind the coffin
of a friend who died of something else.

Gregory and his colleagues in Montevideo
hope to contribute solutions,
work on ways to produce ventilators
and novel disinfection systems
from open source designs.

A grandchild in Paysandú invents
a backyard obstacle course
for her children, my greatgrandchildren,
providing them some small excitement
in this time no one saw coming.

My children are scattered across
a world that is sickening
and dying. We count on Skype,
Facetime, WhatsApp, email and telephone
to keep us close.

Memory Tries to Get Our Attention

Memory wanders the earth in this era
of pandemic and fear.
She whispers stories of past plagues,
reminds us of holocausts
and genocides,
tells us *this too shall pass.*

Memory tries to get our attention
with books, songs, graphs,
even humor, assures us
the friendly touch
we miss today will still
be there tomorrow.

But memory herself is exhausted,
battered by an onslaught
of mixed messages, history books
with missing chapters,
biased news reports
and self-proclaimed scribes.

She insists she's as timely as science
and hope, tries to take her seat
at the table of experts,
get us to see her for who she is
at a time when she knows
she is needed as never before.

Listen to Memory calling.
Ask our elders
for her tales of pain and heroics,
kindness and relevance.
She will take your hand
if you give her yours.

Holograms of Hope

Maps, we know, are drawn
according to their makers'
dreams of grandeur
or humility, lands shaped
by guile or conquest,
vision and gratitude,
in turn informing the minds
of those who teach
their progeny to till
their fields,
plant and reap on them,
sing their songs.

Today we have twin maps:
Los Angeles struggling
beneath pollution's filth
and the same city
under a paler cloud
as traffic deserts
its streets
and people shelter
from this dread virus:
the first blood red,
the second barely washed
in pale pink.

We also have such maps
of Mumbai, Beijing
and other metropoles

that only weeks ago
spewed greenhouse gases
into skies made for wind
and rain, eagles
and clouds.
A dearth of planes also
brings new air, easier
to breathe and kinder
to our lungs.

When social closeness
gives back
the human embrace
and travel puts us
once again hours away
from anywhere else
on earth,
which of these maps
will mirror our cities
and which have
merely been
holograms of hope?

Ying Ying and Lee Lee

Hong Kong's zoo, closed
since the virus struck,
finally provides the intimacy
Ying Ying and Lee Lee need
to mate in peace.

Fourteen long years
their handlers
have urged them
to take advantage
of this moment

that comes only once
every twelve months,
confounding those
cognizant of the pandas'
hormonal peaks.

Their balloon-like bodies
do not find it easy.
Training films and other aids
have failed at demonstrating
the required positions.

The pandas have become
vulnerable to extinction
as some of us are vulnerable
to the virus that's given them
this newfound freedom.

Deterrent to humans, window
of opportunity for pandas:
the world's creatures
accommodate ourselves
to a different time.

Something Will Have to Be Different

Will we wake to the same blue sky,
these canyons displaying a palette
as rich in oranges and mauves,
wild grasses tickling my skin
as they do now?

Will the loaves I take from the oven
taste the same,
their pungency filling the air
with warmth
and sustenance?

Will your eyes smile as they did,
the skin around them
crinkling into lines of joy
mapping all the years
we've loved?

Will we argue the same topics
with equal passion
and conviction,
receive the same answers
to the same questions?

Something will have to be different,
mean what it never meant
before.
Some palpable sign to tell us
we've come through.

If Each Facemask Came with a Poem

If each facemask came with a poem
each bottle of hand gel
with a Brandenburg Concerto
or Sweet Honey belting out
an anthem of hope.
If each pair of latex gloves
was packaged with a favorite painting
left just outside your door.

If every virtual hug could pierce
this worldwide skin of fear,
each six-foot distance between humans
on our lonely walks
reduce to real safety, sure health,
there'd be less room
for the calculated offense flowing
from the president's microphone.

Some insist love is circling the globe
faster than this infection
of invisible droplets
and silent reach of death.
And yes, I feel the love
but also the hate, the hoarding,
the prayer that *as long as it doesn't come
to my house I'll be fine.*

Beloveds: Resist taking refuge
in feelgood lies,
conspiracy theories,
a wrathful God, end times
or the erasure of memory
when what we need now
is science and art
to bring us through to a saner shore.

The Virus as Metaphor

A perfect vehicle for hatred of Others,
some call it the Chinese
or foreign virus:
easy to use tragedy as an excuse
for racism or xenophobia.

I remember the 14th century
when Jews and lepers
were blamed for The Black Death.
Every hater has their moment
in history.

Strange how today's loathers
never evoke those blankets
that carried smallpox and cholera
to the First People
inhabiting our beautiful land.

Mother's Lavender *Ruana*

Wrapping myself in the lavender shawl
that once belonged to Mother
I am in a cocoon,
protected from all threat.

I may have brought this *ruana* from Mexico,
its soft wool surely from sheep
tended lovingly by some shepherd
who also dyed it with love.

I remember Mother wearing this gift
as she wore few others,
though she always told me she loved
what I brought as she loved me.

Mother is long gone. She was spared
the anguish of this virus: fortunate
since the common cold was enough
to send her into terrified retreat.

I pull the shawl about my body and
imagine it a defensive barrier
woven from the wool of Mexican sheep,
exactly what I need today.

Trap a Minute or Two

Yesterday looks different
now that today
has its hands
around our throats.

Tomorrow dissolves
in a haze
of what ifs, its image
pulsing through our veins.

Today looms larger than life
or death, its chorus
of cleaning instructions
devouring time.

Trap a minute or two
to look in the eyes

of those you love and
tell them yes.

Crisis in Present Tense

This is so immense, so overwhelming,
we have not dared ask ourselves
if it or something like it
might return.
Enough to confront
the crisis in present tense.

Did survivors of the Armenian Holocaust
imagine the possibility
three decades later
of Germany's Final Solution?
Those were human-made evils,
this an invisible invasion.

It came. It came, we know not how
or precisely what we did
to pave the way for its arrival.
We cannot say *never again*
as we could about those other horrors.
But then the promise meant nothing then.

The Poet Embraces a Changed World

We have instructions about going out,
social distancing, protective gear.
Don't touch your face, they say,
and wash your hands
for at least 20 seconds
many times a day.

But where are the instructions
about making art
as the virus peers over my shoulder?
How to bring this reality
to a page that stares up
through such uncertainty?

How do I focus my passion
on this poem,
garner the energy
to keep it front and center
obsessed as I am
with the hovering menace.

And how can I share my work
if all the venues
have gone quiet:
publishers' doors are closed,
universities operate virtually
and theaters are empty?

Shelter in place for me must be
shelter inside my art,
claim a new voice
that speaks from within the crisis
to bear witness to what is
and live in an unfamiliar world.

Like a Flower's Pollen

I've stood with the few
against the many,
played my part
in herculean wars
as comrades fell
about me.

I've battled a government
trying to deport me
because it didn't like
what I wrote
or that I was a woman
who wouldn't say I'm sorry.

Going forth in struggle
forward motion
propels
and you do not stop
because movement
is energy.

But this offensive
against the virus
is defensive in nature.
We must shelter in place,
stay calm, resist
in quiet unison.

Our challenge: to build
offensive strength
from defensive posture
like a flower's pollen
when the bee
comes in.

The Sun Will Rise Tomorrow

In a month, thousands more may have died
from this virus invading our lives
but the Road Runner strutting in our patio
will be as curious as always,
the sky's cobalt bowl will be just as blue
and I will love you more than I did yesterday
although not as much as tomorrow.

Cherokee, that ageless woman who wraps
herself in her frayed blanket and hunkers
in the warmth of a neighborhood doorway
will still avert her eyes when they
bring her morning coffee from the cafe
forced to limit its hours but that hasn't stopped
caring about those who live in its radius.

Cherokee's days and nights are the same
with or without this crisis,
her winters just as cold,
her summers as hot, and her hunger
as dependent on the kindness of strangers
worried now about what this pandemic
has in store.

My Italian friend says his parents back home
haven't left their house in weeks.
In Toulouse my granddaughter's restaurant

is shuttered and she and her Moroccan partner
remain secluded. A grandson in Melbourne
has lost his job because China, for now,
has stopped shipping what the company sells.

In her megalomania, Nicaragua's vice-president
urges her compatriots to make merry,
hug and kiss. *Love in a time of COVID-19*, she cries
as she claims exceptionality from God
and revels in a power that can kill.
Dictatorship is especially dangerous
on pandemic's wings.

But the red rock canyon is red as ever
and exudes its desert heat.
The finch that accompanies our breakfast
returns as always to the branch
outside our window. You take my hand
and tell me the sun will rise tomorrow,
the day after and the one after that.

Welcome the Next Clear Breath

She plays the soundtrack from Three
Billboards Outside Ebbing Missouri
and I realize music's gift
to lift my spirits.

I read again how some say this
is God's punishment
for gay rights or trans people
or letting foreigners

into this pure white land of ours,
and I wonder how anyone
can love a god so vindictive
or contemptuous of humanity.

Not God but all of us: the Thai elephant
trainer, banker in Manhattan and
teacher in Mexico, must move together
against this plague.

We must stay at home, if we have one,
and when we venture out
keep our social distance from one another,
wash our hands, wear masks,

check on family and friends, especially
the elderly who may need
a hand as infection swirls about us
and we wait to welcome

the next clear breath, loved one's step,
birdcall or new green leaf and sun
coming up over the mountains
to the east.

Blue or Pink

Preteen Johnny begs for ContraVirus,
the videogame with variations.
He can install the program
for Spanish Flu, Zika
or COVID-19
though all the cool kids
play the latter.

Sister Jenny wants Coronavirus
Nurse Kit
with its miniature alcohol swabs,
facemasks and gloves.
She will minister to her dolls,
keeping them safe
until the danger passes.

If these children of the future
still play blue or pink,
their games of choice
gendered as all infected lives,
this crisis will have taught us
nothing about pandemics
or anything else.

Spiral

We are learning a new language,
virtual pronunciation
we practice daily

absent the spoken word
in this era
of discordant isolation.

We have time, all the time
in the world
until we have none.

If the pandemic moves
in spiral,
all the graphs are wrong.

All the statistics are beliefs
we hardly remember
as the virus comes to stay.

To learn to think in spiral
means ridding ourselves
of arrogance:

We are no safer than, no better
than, no whiter
or more citizen than.

Divesting ourselves of covert pride
we ride the spiral
to a wiser place.

Eighty Times More

We now know the first person with
COVID-19 was in Wuhan, China
on December 1, 2019. A place
we didn't think about before.

One hundred twenty days to date, at first
not perceived as exceptional and then
entering our consciousness
with the force of every lie and truth.

Forty thousand have died from the virus
in this time of worldwide crisis.
But they are not the only deaths
we record in these 120 days.

In the same period, close to three million
(80 times more) have died of hunger,
1.2 million (33 times more) because they
had no access to medical care.

Ninety-six thousand (two and a half
times more) women died
from lack of rudimentary attention
giving birth and 672,000 infants

(18.1 times more) were born dead
for the same reason.
Statistics can be suspect but there is
only one way to interpret these.

This is not about subtraction but addition,
not to minimize the Corona deaths
but also consider these others
on which we've turned our backs.

Death from hunger is as slow and painful
as lungs filling with bloody fluid
in a world where none of these atrocities
need happen.

The Pandemic Picks and Chooses

One is confined to a light and airy home
and well-stocked pantry,
another to a damp basement
or homeless tent.

One sits before her computer screen
delighting at the day's explosion
of hilarity spawned
by this deadly plague.

Another cannot escape an uncle's
treacherous hand or father's
belt: their personal quarantine
of waking nightmare.

One bemoans his inability to work
from home, while his neighbor
suits up for her hospital shift
with tears in her eyes.

We are all in this together but
are not the same.
Like all attackers the pandemic
picks and chooses.

David against Invading Goliath

—for Lincoln Bergman

Today I hear Vietnam will send 450,000
protective medical gowns
to the United States, a country
that a half century ago
bombed its cities, napalmed its people
and chemically poisoned its fields.

I am old enough to remember the war
that shaped my generation,
revere a country
where partisans on bicycles
resisted the greatest army on earth
and prevailed.

Passion for homeland and freedom
created a David
against the invading Goliath.
Decades have passed. Veterans on both sides
have reconciled and in this crisis
compassion emerges from the night.

Now the story has a sequel in which
David is concerned
for Goliath's welfare. Winning
wasn't all that mattered and Vietnam's gift
is commerce and imagination
in perfect synchrony.

The virus spreads with every breath
on every continent, but if
we can see one another as humans
solidarity will travel faster,
live longer, change a future
we'll be proud to inhabit.

Remember Your Eyes

Will we shake hands again? Maybe not.
Where people touch noses or foreheads
in greeting, alternate habits must emerge
as precaution against contagion.

Even when the virus has been forced into
deep retreat, a kiss on both cheeks may
exist in memory only and the sequence
of three would be senseless risk.

Hugs will be out of the question, and
that long embrace once measuring
depth of feeling will scream danger
written in pulsing lights.

Social habits usually change as each
generation becomes more relaxed
than the one before. These habits
trend in the opposite direction.

But we must not allow virtual touch
to take the place of every human
interaction. Remember: your eyes
can search out other eyes.

Some Questions in a Time of Crisis

Will the world be cleaner when this virus
has finally gone
to where all infection gives up and dies?
So much swabbing with alcohol wipes,
so much washing of hands.

Will we see more or maybe just better
when we turn our heads
and can look at one another
like the woman in her burqa
proficient in the language of sight?

Like the dolphins and swans coming home
to Venice's canals, will we welcome
a return of wildlife
to all those places once congested
by our invasion of their space?

Will we have learned that kindness
must replace avarice and
that it's up to us
to plant justice in those wild gardens
overrun by the weeds of hate?

What will have changed? What remain
the same?
Will those who survive
remember or forget, move forward
or keep on sheltering in broken place?

When the Crisis is Over

In times of crisis we always say
things will be different
after this or
this must never be allowed
to happen again.

Fast-forward a couple of months.
The crisis is over for now,
and we can take walks,
see our friends,
begin to rebuild our lives.

Slowly, too slowly for many,
life resumes its routine.
But the lessons
we might have taken to heart
crouch in the White House

basement, in Congress
and boardrooms,
tired of begging our attention.
aghast at being swept
under the rug yet again.

ABOUT THE AUTHOR

Margaret Randall is a feminist poet, writer, photographer and social activist. She is the author of over 150 books. She is the recipient of the 2019 Haydée Santamaría Medal from Casa de las Americas in Havana, and the prestigious 2019 Poet of Two Hemispheres Prize, presented by Ecuador's Poesía en Paralelo Cero. In 2017, she was awarded the Medal of Literary Merit by Literatura en el Bravo, Chihuahua, Mexico. The University of New Mexico granted her an honorary doctorate in letters in 2019. In 2020 she was given the George Garrett Award by AWP.

Born in New York City in 1936, she has lived for extended periods in Albuquerque, New York, Seville, Mexico City, Havana, and Managua. Shorter stays in Peru and North Vietnam were also formative. In the 1960s, with Sergio Mondragón she founded and co-edited *El Corno Emplumado / The Plumed Horn*, a bilingual literary journal which for eight years published some of the most dynamic and meaningful writing of an era. Robert Cohen took over when Mondragón left the publication in 1968. From 1984 through 1994 she taught at a number of U.S. universities.

Randall was privileged to live among New York's abstract expressionists in the 1950s and early '60s, participate in the Mexican student movement of 1968, share important years of the Cuban revolution (1969-1980), the first three years of Nicaragua's Sandinista project (1980-1984), and visit North Vietnam during the heroic last months of the U.S. American war in that country (1974). Her four children—Gregory, Sarah, Ximena and Ana—have given her ten grandchildren and two great-grandchildren. She has lived with her life companion, the painter and teacher Barbara Byers, for the past 34 years.

Upon her return to the United States from Nicaragua in 1984, Randall was ordered to be deported when the government invoked the 1952 McCarran-Walter Immigration and Nationality Act, judging opinions expressed in some of her books to be "against the good order and happiness of the United States." The Center for Constitutional Rights defended Randall, and many writers and others joined in an almost five-year battle for reinstatement of citizenship. She won her case in 1989.

In 1990 Randall was awarded the Lillian Hellman and Dashiell Hammett grant for writers victimized by political repression. In 2004 she was the first recipient of PEN New Mexico's Dorothy Doyle Lifetime Achievement Award for Writing and Human Rights Activism.

Recent non-fiction books by Randall include *To Change the World: My Life in Cuba* (Rutgers University Press), *More Than Things* (University of Nebraska Press), *Che On My Mind,* and *Haydée Santamaría, Cuban Revolutionary: She Led by Transgression* (both from Duke University Press). Her most recent nonfiction works are *Only the Road / Solo el Camino: Eight Decades of Cuban Poetry* (Duke University Press, 2016) and *Exporting Revolution: Cuba's Global Solidarity* (Duke University Press, 2017).

"The Unapologetic Life of Margaret Randall" is an hour-long documentary by Minneapolis filmmakers Lu Lippold and Pam Colby. It is distributed by Cinema Guild in New York City.

Randall's most recent collections of poetry and photographs are *Their Backs to the Sea* (2009), *My Town: A Memoir of Albuquerque, New Mexico* (2010), *As If the Empty Chair: Poems for the Disappeared / Como si la silla vacía: poemas para los desaparecidos* (2011), *Where Do We Go from Here?* (2012), *Daughter of Lady Jaguar Shark* (2013), *The Rhizome as a Field of Broken Bones* (2013), *About Little Charlie Lindbergh and other Poems* (2014), *Beneath a Trespass of Sorrow* (2014), *Bodies / Shields* (2015), *She Becomes Time* (2016), *The Morning After: Poetry and Prose in a Post-Truth World* (2017), and *Against Atrocity* (2019), all published by Wings Press. *Time's Language: Selected Poems (1959-2018)* was published by Wings Press in 2018. Many of Randall's collections of poetry have been published in Spanish translations throughout the hemisphere.

Among Randall's most recent books, her memoir *I Never Left Home: Poet, Feminist, Revolutionary* was published by Duke University Press, and a companion volume, *My Life in 100 Objects* came out from New Village Press, both in 2020.

Colophon

This first edition of *Starfish on a Beach: The Pandemic Poems*, by Margaret Randall, has been printed on 55 pound "natural" paper containing a percentage of recycled fiber. Titles have been set in Aquiline Two, Charlemagne, and Caslon Bold type, the text in Adobe Caslon type. This book was designed by Bryce Milligan.

On-line catalogue and ordering:
www.wingspress.com
Wings Press titles are distributed to the trade by the
Independent Publishers Group
www.ipgbook.com
and in Europe by Gazelle
www.gazellebookservices.co.uk

Also available as an ebook.

*For more information about Margaret Randall,
visit her website at www.margaretrandall.org.*